IMPORTANT JOBS
ON FILM SETS

by Mari Bolte

a Capstone company — publishers for children

Raintree is an imprint of Capstone Global Library Limited, a company incorporated in England and Wales having its registered office at 264 Banbury Road, Oxford, OX2 7DY – Registered company number: 6695582

www.raintree.co.uk
myorders@raintree.co.uk

Hardback edition text © Capstone Global Library Limited 2024
Paperback edition text © Capstone Global Library Limited 2025

The moral rights of the proprietor have been asserted. All rights reserved. No part of this publication may be reproduced in any form or by any means (including photocopying or storing it in any medium by electronic means and whether or not transiently or incidentally to some other use of this publication) without the written permission of the copyright owner, except in accordance with the provisions of the Copyright, Designs and Patents Act 1988 or under the terms of a licence issued by the Copyright Licensing Agency, 5th Floor, Shackleton House, 4 Battle Bridge Lane, London, SE1 2HX (www.cla.co.uk). Applications for the copyright owner's written permission should be addressed to the publisher.

British Library Cataloguing in Publication Data
A full catalogue record for this book is available from the British Library.

ISBN 978 1 3982 5088 8 (hardback)
ISBN 978 1 3982 5089 5 (paperback)

Editor: Mandy R. Robbins
Designer: Dina Her
Media researcher: Jo Miller
Production specialist: Tori Abraham

Originated by Capstone Global Library Ltd

Acknowledgements
Alamy: Agencja Fotograficzna Caro, 6, Eamon O'Doherty, 17, Entertainment Pictures, 21, PictureLux/The Hollywood Archive, 9, ZUMA Press, Inc., 27; Getty Images: Geber86, 14, John Eder, 5; Newscom: Splash News, 18; Shutterstock: DC Studio, Cover (bottom), Frame Stock Footage, 22, Gorgev, 13, Gorodenkoff, 10, 25, guruXOX, 28, pui_bunny, Cover (top left), Sergey Novikov, Cover (top right)

Every effort has been made to contact copyright holders of material reproduced in this book. Any omissions will be rectified in subsequent printings if notice is given to the publisher.

All the internet addresses (URLs) given in this book were valid at the time of going to press. However, due to the dynamic nature of the internet, some addresses may have changed, or sites may have changed or ceased to exist since publication. While the author and publisher regret any inconvenience this may cause readers, no responsibility for any such changes can be accepted by either the author or the publisher.

Printed and bound in India

CONTENTS

On the big screen 4
Actors 7
Special effects artists 8
Directors 11
Producers 12
Writers 15
Set designers 16
Craft services 19
Animal trainers 20
Animators 23
Composers 26

    Other jobs on a film set 29
    Glossary 30
    Find out more 31
    Index 32
    About the author 32

Words in **bold** are in the glossary.

ON THE BIG SCREEN

Who doesn't love a good film? The comedy, the action, the drama! Watch them in a cinema. Press play at home. Or take them anywhere with a phone. But films don't just make themselves!

Many people work together to make films. Find out what they do. Every job is important!

ACTORS

Actors are the people you see on the screen. They bring the characters to life. Sometimes they do action scenes. They train hard to get into shape.

Acting is more than reading lines off a page. Actors must work with other actors. They can show a character's thoughts or feelings. Being funny or good at singing or dancing are other ways to act. Actors can be any age, **gender**, race or physical ability.

SPECIAL EFFECTS ARTISTS

Special effects artists make imaginary things seem real. Robots that run on wheels or spaceships that fly are special effects. Special effects artists make tiny **sets** that look like actual places.

Artists use computers too. They can make imaginary creatures. They can even make explosions! A good artist can make anything a film might need.

FACT
Superhero films are expensive to make. Each Marvel film costs between about £80 million and £210 million. *Avengers: Endgame* cost about £300 million!

DIRECTORS

Directors are in charge of the creative parts of a film. Only they know what they want the film to look like. They make sure the **script** makes sense. They choose actors. They help the actors understand the story.

The film needs to stay on **budget** and on time. That is the director's job too. A good director is organized. They are also good at working with people.

PRODUCERS

Producers are the people who get films made. Sometimes they come up with new ideas. Sometimes they read scripts and pick their favourites. They also find a way to pay for the film.

If the director needs more money, the producers get it. If people do not agree, they find a solution. Good producers are problem solvers.

FACT

Sometimes, actors are also producers. They might want to work on new or different types of projects. Or they might just like to make films.

WRITERS

A film is only as good as its script. Most of your favourite lines in films are thanks to a writer. A writer can make a book into a film. Or they might have a brand-new idea. Sometimes they turn a bad script into a good one.

Writers can work alone or together. It might take more than one writer to come up with a film script.

SET DESIGNERS

Sets are where films are filmed. A set might include a room or a building. Everything in that room is part of the set. A set designer makes sure the set looks like the real thing. They choose items that belong in that space. Every wall, piece of furniture or decoration you see in a film scene is planned by the set designer.

Sometimes, the cameras move. A set designer makes sure you never see anything that doesn't belong.

CRAFT SERVICES

Making films can take months. It is hard work! People making the film must eat. Leaving the set to get food wastes time. Craft services has food ready at all times. They set out tables.

Crew members can stop for a snack or a meal. If a film is being shot in the desert, craft services supplies plenty of cold water to drink. They also clean up any mess left by people.

ANIMAL TRAINERS

Some films use animals. Actors might ride horses. They could have a pet. Dangerous animals add drama.

Trainers teach animals what to do. The animals learn where to stand. A dog will bark when the trainer tells it to. Some animals can do tricks. They carry items. They jump over things. Good film animals behave while on set. When animals work well with their trainers, the film is easier to make.

ANIMATORS

Animators draw creatures and bring them to life on screen. Most use computers for this. They might create a made-up being. It needs to look real next to a person.

Sometimes, the whole film must be drawn. This is the case with cartoon films. Animators work with directors and designers. They try to make sure every detail is right.

Some films are shot in front of a green screen. The actors pretend action is happening around them. But, really, they are in a room painted green. Later, animators add in backgrounds and objects. The backgrounds cover everything green. It can look like actors are in another country or even on another planet.

Bright neon green is usually used. That's because few things are that colour. Nothing the actor wears can match the green screen. It wouldn't show up if it did!

COMPOSERS

A film's story is important. But so is the music! Music helps you know when to feel happy or sad. It adds excitement. When something scary is about to happen, you will know.

A good **composer** writes music that matches what is happening on-screen. Did you leave the cinema humming music from the film? Then the composer was good!

FACT

John Williams is a famous film composer. You have probably heard his music before! He has worked on film series such as Jurassic Park, Star Wars and Harry Potter.

There are many people needed to make a film. The things you see, hear and feel are thanks to filmmakers. Everyone needs to work together. If one part is not done well, the whole film is not a success. Would you want to work on a film set? What job would you do?

OTHER JOBS ON A FILM SET

Camera operators

A camera operator sets up the camera equipment. Then they record everything. Camera operators make sure the shots stay clear and the actors are easily seen.

Costume designers

Costumes tell audiences a lot about the film. They reveal details about the characters too. They can show where and when a film takes place. Costume designers help bring characters to life.

Grips

Film cameras are heavy. Grips carry this heavy equipment. They also put the equipment together and look after it.

GLOSSARY

animator someone who creates cartoons or realistic art with characters that seem to be moving

budget plan for spending and saving money

composer person who writes songs or music

crew team of people who work together

gender sex that a person identifies as (typically male or female)

script story for a play, film or television programme

set stage scene where the action is taking place, such as the kitchen or even on a mountaintop

FIND OUT MORE

BOOKS

Shoot Epic Short Documentaries (Make a Movie!), Thomas Kingsley Troupe (Raintree, 2020)

Write Your Own Scripts, Andrew Prentice (Usborne, 2020)

WEBSITES

www.bbc.co.uk/bitesize/articles/z7t27nb
Find out more about the different jobs in film.

www.bbc.co.uk/bitesize/articles/zjrtxbk
Try these filmmaking actiities on the BBC Bitesize website.

www.twinkl.co.uk/homework-help/art-music-design-homework-help/drama-theatre-and-film-facts-for-kids/more-fascinating-film-facts-for-kids
Learn some fun facts about filmmaking on this website.

INDEX

actors 7, 11, 13, 20, 24, 29
animal trainers 20
animators 23, 24
Avengers: Endgame 8

budgets 11

camera operators 29
cameras 16, 29
composers 26, 27
   Williams, John 27
computers 8, 23
costume designers 29
craft services 19

directors 11, 12, 23
green screens 24
grips 29

music 26, 27

producers 12, 13

scripts 11, 12, 15
set designers 16
sets 8, 16
special effects artists 8

writers 15

ABOUT THE AUTHOR

Mari Bolte is an author and editor of children's books on all sorts of subjects, from graphic novels about science to art projects to hands-on history. She lives in Minnesota, USA, in the middle of a forest full of animals.